Sid's tin

A fat rat sits
in the sun.

Sid hops up
on the log.

The rat runs.
Sid runs.

The rat pops into a tin.

It is Sid's tin.

Sid taps his tin
and it tips.

The fat rat runs.
But not Sid!
Sid hugs his tin.

Before reading

Say the sounds: g o b h e r f u l

Practise blending the sounds: Sid's tin fat rat sits sun Sid hops log runs pops taps tips hugs

High-frequency words: a in up on it but not
Tricky words: the into is his and
Vocabulary check: pops – in this book, this word means "goes"

Story discussion: What is Sid doing in the cover picture? How do you think he feels about his tin?

Teaching points: Check that children can say the phonemes /g/ /o/ /b/ /h/ /r/ /f/ /u/ /l/, and that they can identify the grapheme that goes with each phoneme.
Check that they understand Sid's feelings and why they change during the story.
Check that children can identify and read the tricky words: the, into, is, his, and.

After reading

Comprehension:
- Where is the rat at the start of the story?
- Who chases the rat?
- Why do you think the rat pops into Sid's tin?
- What happens to the rat at the end of the story?

Fluency: Speed-read the words again from the inside front cover.